Letts Guides to Sugarcraft

Arranging
Floral Sprays

MARIE HERBSTRITT

CONSULTANT: NICHOLAS LODGE

CHARLES LETTS · *Letts* · FOUNDED 1796

DEDICATION

For Bob, Chris and Matthew, with love

Designed and Edited by
Anness Publishing Limited
4a The Old Forge
7 Caledonian Road
London N1 9DX

First published 1991
by Charles Letts & Co Ltd
Diary House, Borough Road
London SE1 1DW

Reprinted 1991, 1992

© 1991 Charles Letts & Co Ltd

ISBN 1–85238–138–8

British Library Cataloguing in Publication Data
Herbstritt, Marie
    Arranging floral sprays – (Letts guides to sugarcraft)
    1. Flowers. Arrangement
    I. Title
    745.92

'Letts' is a registered trademark of
Charles Letts (Scotland) Ltd.

Editorial Director: Joanna Lorenz
Designer: Mike Snell
Photographer: Sue Atkinson

Printed and bound in Italy

ACKNOWLEDGEMENTS

The author wishes to thank the following:
Barbara Everett for all the private tuition in floristry techniques and for never letting me down; Sandy Israel and Elizabeth in Euless, Texas, for being there for me at the beginning, for giving me many opportunities in the USA and for providing so much encouragement; Adrian Westrope for his generosity in allowing me to use his lace pattern, for creating a unique side design for the long octagonal Christmas cake on page 84 and for his support and friendship; Anne Shaw for beautiful stargazer lilies and for being my teacher from the beginning – thank you for sharing so much!; Sue Cliff and Adrian Westrope for making the mountains of flower (gum) paste needed, keeping me in constant supply; Linda Hudson, my sister, for the hours and hours of loving babysitting and for designing and knitting a beautiful mohair cardigan especially for me; All my sisters, Amoulla, Linda, Jackie and Helen, and their families, for giving constant support and inspiration; Malcolm Craig – a special thank you for trust in my abilities unseen, in putting me in the right place at the right time; Cortina Butler, Gary Chapman and Nick Lodge for believing in me; Char Brown at the Maid of Scandinavia for being the first to publish my work in Mailbox News in the USA and for continued interest in me; Cake Art, Sugarcraft Supplies Ltd, CH Offray and Sons Ltd, Hammilworth Floral Products Ltd, JF Renshaw Ltd, Cel Cakes and Royal Crown Derby/Royal Doulton for supplying materials, equipment and props; Debra Shaw at Cake Decor, Derby, for all her help.

Contents

Foreword

Floral Sprays is among the first in a new series of guides to sugarcraft, and is a must for any cake decorator's library.

Although there have been many books on the market in recent years with sections on how to arrange sugar flowers into sprays, this book is the only one to devote itself entirely to spray design, presenting the subject in much greater detail than ever before. Marie Herbstritt has designed not only a wonderful collection of practical design projects for all occasions, but clearly describes all the basic principles of sugar flower arranging. Classic shapes, such as the crescent, round and Hogarth curve, are included as well as the more unusual arrangements, such as teardrop and freestyle.

Floral Sprays is packed full of many different projects for you to follow, from the grandest bridal bouquet to a simple Victorian posy. Each arrangement provides a quick guide to all the components necessary to create the display, so that you know exactly how many of each leaf and flower you will need. Together with the step-by-step photographs and easy-to-read directions, you can be assured of perfect results every time.

Marie and I have known each other for several years. We always meet up at major exhibitions and conferences in the USA and UK and I have been continually impressed by her colourful and innovative style of cake decorating. I am confident that you will enjoy working your way through this wonderful book and will soon be inventing new floral spray arrangements of your own.

Nicholas Lodge

Introduction

This is not a book about making flowers or piped designs. It is a guide about how to put together the flowers you have made, into traditional and unusual arrangements. There are already many books and classes that give instruction on making your own flowers, designing cakes, piping in royal icing and the many other facets of cake decorating. This book is designed to help you know what to do with the flowers once you

have made them! I know that many of my readers can already make exquisite flowers but still need guidance on how to structure and display them. Similarly, this book aims to help those of you who are just embarking on the sugar flower adventure to bring your first flowers to life by following the presentation guidelines offered here.

Flower arranging is a craft where your skills expand with every flower you make and every arrangement you put together. The variety of shapes, colours and styles of flowers and arrangements is limitless, and you will develop your own style. No two people make flowers exactly the same and everyone interprets their arrangements differently. The size of your flowers may be smaller or larger than mine; your choice of colour will of course be dependent on the project you are working on and your interpretation of it. So your final pieces may look considerably different to those in this book, but as long as you abide by the general guidelines offered, they should always be pleasing to the eye.

All flower arranging is an art form, whether you are working with fresh, silk, paper or sugar flowers, and as such one can only give guidelines and general techniques because, in the end, it is your creation. You always impart your own personality and style when making sugar flowers and arranging them. Nobody can tell you that what you do is wrong, because it is a personal creation and that is what is so satisfying about this absorbing hobby. The displays given here are not the only methods and shapes of arrangements: there are thousands of freestyle variations and endless different means of presentation, but I chose to stay with traditional shapes because this will give you a starting point from which to grow and develop your own more adventurous themes.

In this book, alongside the sugarcraft advice, I share with you information and guidelines that I have myself learnt from working alongside a florist. If the floral side of cake decorating is where your interest lies, then I suggest you try a class in floral arranging as well as the practical side of flower making. If you are lucky, there will be night classes in your area.

Sharing these techniques with you has made me realise how much I love the craft of sugar flower arranging. I hope that you find in this book the instruction you need to develop your hobby, but also I trust you will have much fun with this stimulating pastime and enjoy much reward for your labours!

Marie Herbstritt

General Rules

Arranging sugarpaste flowers is different in many ways to arranging fresh or silk flowers. Since we can make our own blooms, we can take many liberties with size, colour and shape. When scaling a design up or down in size, we can make flowers to fit. For example, we can make really small arum lilies to accompany larger roses. We could if we wanted make a yellow sweet pea, and of course, we can make endless combinations of 'fantasy flowers'. The point is that for this particular craft, it is not necessary to follow literally the rules for fresh flower arranging given in books on that subject.

Although I often use many ingredients in my arrangements, I like clean simple lines with plenty of detail within the arrangement to interest the onlooker. I find then that the cakes look stunning from a distance so that people want to get closer and inspect the floral arrangement; then, once there, they find plenty of fine detail and are usually thrilled with the final result!

The stems of sugar flowers are rigid and therefore any movement is not as nature would intend, but that which we put there ourselves. Of course, to create the illusion, we try to copy Mother Nature as much as possible. The better we are at this, the more natural our arrangements will look.

We can take some guidelines from fresh flower work, as far as shape of arrangement, proportional use of size and complementary colours are concerned, and we can apply a few useful rules and tips to help us achieve our own desired effect.

On the whole, we are usually trying to create a realistic piece of work and so use colours which are copied from nature. This does not mean to say that using artistic licence to make something new and different is wrong.

No arrangement described in this book is intended to be eaten. All the flowers are arranged on wire and some have artificial stamens, which make them unsafe to eat. Also, most are highly coloured and would be unpalatable if eaten. I consider the arrangements to be for decorative purposes only.

COLOUR

It is always a good idea to use various shades of a main colour to give your work perspective. We have all been taught to lighten rose petals as we move from the centre petals to the outer ones, to give the flower a more realistic appearance. It is the same with your arrangements. No two flowers are exactly the same shape or colour, so vary slightly the shade of colour that you use to make each flower, to create a very beautiful overall effect. Once you have put your flowers into an arrangement, the light will fall on each in a different way – your display will bring your flowers to life.

Take into consideration the part that various colours can play in your work:

- Reds are bold and positive. They will appear to come forward in an arrangement.
- Blues will recede as they are introverted colours.
- Yellows will elevate and light up an arrangement. They go very well with blues.
- Orange is a hard colour, but when mixed with browns, yellows and greens can give a very warm and striking effect.
- Violet shades diminish in an arrangement.
- Pastel shades – soft pinks, blues, mauves, lavenders and creamy yellows – are always a delight when mixed with light foliage, and seldom fail to please.
- Green is a neutral colour and foliage makes a wonderful background or base.

Right: Subtle use of edible colourings can give you an enormous range of beautiful shades to arrange into sprays.

Monochromic

Mono means one, therefore a monochromic arrangement is a design of one colour. Once you have decided which colour to work with, it's a good idea to look up which flowers come in that colour and then decide which to make.

You need to make the flowers using different tints and shades of the single colour you have chosen. The main contrast in such an arrangement will be that of texture, for example, shiny rose leaves, fluffy carnations, ruffled roses and sweet peas, and waxy arum lilies.

Monochromic colour schemes are considered to be harmonious and soothing. You should choose a colour appropriate to the occasion for which it is designed, of course.

Complementary

Complementary colours are those which are directly opposite each other on the colour wheel, such as yellow and violet, blue and orange, or green and scarlet.

By using tints and tones of these colour pairs, you can produce very pleasant results.

Harmonic

Groups of three or four colours lying next to each other on the colour wheel also work well together, for example, pale yellow, peach and orange.

Triadic

Any three colours lying at equidistant intervals on the colour wheel are contrasting colours, quite different in themselves but working well together. Examples of these are blue, red and yellow, or violet, orange and green.

SCALE

It is important to give some thought to the scale of your flowers. If you are trying to achieve a realistic look in your project, you will need to make your flowers to scale, although not necessarily to size. For example, if your particular finished rose is 2.5–4cm (1–1½″) in diameter, it's no use making filler flowers of the same diameter! Of course this would not look right. But if you make filler flowers the size of a pinhead, this would also look unrealistic. The flower cutters generally available to us do tend to be proportional however, which helps considerably.

You should vary the sizes of the flowers within a spray, in order to give some contrast and detail to your work; sprays made entirely of the same-sized flowers can be most uninteresting. The arrangement as a whole must also be in scale with the chosen setting: work your arrangements according to the size and shape of your cake, container or setting. A tall arrangement or large-scale flowers would look silly in a tiny pastillage card setting, for example.

SHAPE

When deciding what style of arrangement to make, you have to take into consideration the final setting for your work. For the top of a cake, you will need an all-round arrangement which can be viewed from all sides. For the sides of a cake, this is unnecessary as it will be backed by the cake, so symmetrical and asymmetrical shapes are most useful for this position.

Should you wish to use a round shape for the side of a cake, it would of course have to use the side of the cake as its base and would need a lot of room — both width and height. Similarly, symmetrical and asymmetrical shapes are quite difficult to use as top decorations. You would have to ensure that some flowers were placed around the back, in line with the rest of the arrangement.

Aside from the actual shape of the arrangement, you need to consider the shape of the flowers you will be using. Roses, carnations and chrysanthemums are all round in shape and as such are quite easy to place in an arrangement. Orchids, lilies and the like are, however, rather more difficult to arrange, as their shape is rather spread out and not massed in the centre. They are also easily broken so supreme care should be taken.

Essential to your work are items with a pointed

shape. For example, a variety of buds, leaves and foliage are important in the formation of the overall shape of your arrangement and also give a more realistic look to your work, particularly with the foliage. Your arrangement will be enhanced by using a combination of these various shapes in your work.

The basic rule for all arrangements, whether they are wired or arranged, is first and foremost to define your shape. To achieve a clear defined shape, you first create an outline. This is why the use of leaves is so important. Use the tips of your leaves as your line and position them accordingly to create your shape. Do not go beyond this line, but keep within its perimeter at all times. By using leaves as a backdrop to your arrangements, you are giving the work a natural setting – a beautiful transition to your cake.

Position your main flowers in the centre of the arrangement, offset from each other, in a zigzag pattern if you wish. These flowers are the main feature and focal point of the arrangement. If you were to place open roses at the points and small buds in the centre, you would not see the full beauty of your hard work and the shape would be lost. If you are graduating your sizes, graduate upwards towards the centre. When working any arrangement, remember too to carry the main colour to all the points. This can be achieved with the use of coloured buds, blossom sprays, filler flowers or ribbon loops.

HEIGHT

The height of your arrangement is decided by the positioning of the central main flower or flowers. These must all be kept on the same level, and nothing should overshadow your main flowers except perhaps a ribbon loop which may be a whisper higher. One other exception to this could be gypsophila or any ornaments like wired pearls which are used as accessories and do not detract from the focal point of the arrangement.

The depth is achieved by recessing the filler flowers. If all your flowers remain on the same level, the impact of your main flowers will be lost. By putting the filler flowers lower than the main flowers, you give the latter their 'own space'; the arrangement is given depth and all the flowers are shown at their best.

SPACE

Space is a very important element in your work. Each flower must have its own space – do not overcrowd! Also, be careful not to overdo the number of arrangements on one cake, and keep your display in proportion to its container or vase if you are using one. A rule of thumb is, when using a tall vase, do not bring your arrangement more than two thirds of the way down, and avoid letting it touch the base of the vase. When using other types of container, stick to the ratio of two thirds flowers, one third empty container, to achieve a sense of proportion and balance.

Wherever possible, use an odd number of main flowers as this gives balance to your arrangement – this has been an important guideline for florists for many years.

Keep your flowers well spaced, and do not press them in too close together. Take a look, for instance, at some of the work with orchids (pages 58 and 70) as these are particularly awkward to arrange. The very fact that the petals are wired separately is one of the reasons that this flower looks so lifelike. However, because the petals are so spread out, the flower needs to be fitted particularly carefully into an arrangement, and given its own space. If it were packed in too tightly with the other flowers, it would look cramped, you probably would not be able to see it in its entirety and the hard work you had put into making the flower would have been wasted. Also, you would be putting your flowers at greater risk of breakage. I am told that in modern floristry, enough space should be left in an arrangement for 'the butterflies to fly through'!

often designed to cut the tape too thinly. The simplest method is to take a fabric cutter or sharp knife and cut the tape in half on the roll. By doing this, you can work with the tape directly from the roll and do not have to keep interrupting the flow of your work to cut tape.

Using wire

When making your flowers initially, there is no way you are going to know how long to cut the wires. Personally, I cut the standard lengths of the covered wires used in sugarcraft into 4 equal pieces, sometimes 5. However, when assembling your arrangement, you may find that you need to have either a longer or shorter wire.

I do not make the flowers on wire 20 or 23cm (8 or 9″) long initially, but simply tape an extra length of wire onto the flower wire as and when it is needed. That way, I find there is less risk of breakage when the flowers are drying in the oasis. Adding wire is also done to add strength to a flower.

When arranging flowers into an oasis of paste, you will find that you need to shorten the wires. Sometimes you will need to cut off quite a large proportion of the wire to get your flower to sit correctly in the paste. Do not be afraid to do this as you should never insert wire directly into your cake.

Using ribbon loops and trails

When making the ribbon loops for a project, scale them to the size of the piece you are doing.

Choose colours to highlight your project and give it that final lift. For example, the gold ribbons in the Christmas arrangement (page 84) give the whole project a final flourish. They do not detract from the foliage, but still manage to 'leap out and hit you between the eyes'. They complement the arrangement, and that is the only role your ribbons should play. Remember, it is the flowers which are important, even if they are your first attempts. People will always appreciate the efforts you have put into them and would rather see them showcased than a huge array of ribbons.

While on this theme, I should point out that it is just as easy to overdo stamens in the same way. It is not a good idea to use huge amounts of long stamens everywhere; it has the same effect as too much ribbon.

Ribbons can be looped for flower arranging in a variety of ways. In this book I have used:
– The single loop
– The single loop with tail
– The ribbon trails to finish off posies and bouquets
– Ribbon bows

Ribbon is also a traditional trim for the side of a cake, sometimes culminating in a bow. For a perfect finishing touch, edge the cakeboard with ribbon complementary in colour to your flower arrangement. This carries your colour down and gives a wonderful overall professional effect.

DISPLAYING ARRANGEMENTS

The simplest way of putting flowers on a cake is to tape or wire them together and simply lay them on the cake. The spray can be fixed to the cake with a dab of royal icing if appropriate. Obviously, if the cake has to be transported to its destination, it can be boxed in a separate container from the decoration. In this case, it would need to be reassembled in situ, but this would probably not present any great difficulty. I prefer not to fix the decoration to the cake as then the risk of damage is minimized.

An alternative is to wire together a spray or arrangement and place it into a container or holder of some sort, to be placed on top of the cake. An example of this is the traditional silver vase for the top of a wedding cake. Nowadays, manufacturers are producing some exquisite flower containers in perspex (plexiglass) which have been specially designed for this purpose.

Yet another method is to arrange your flowers in some flower (gum) paste or sugarpaste and fix this directly onto the cake. Once the arrangement has been made, the paste will set and the arrangement can be placed or removed as a whole unit. If you

Ribbon loops and trails

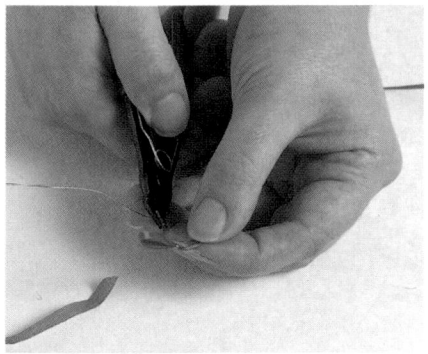

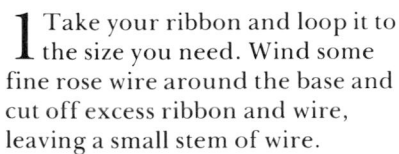

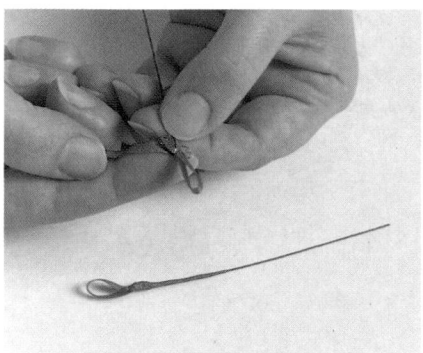

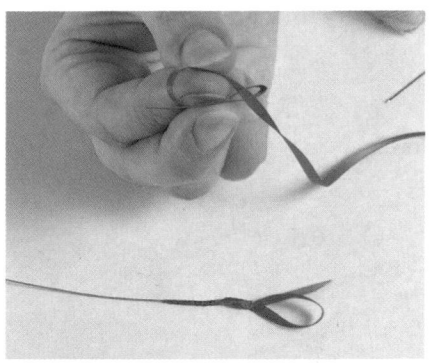

1 Take your ribbon and loop it to the size you need. Wind some fine rose wire around the base and cut off excess ribbon and wire, leaving a small stem of wire.

2 Tape the base of this to a longer, stronger wire, say 26 gauge or 28 gauge. The length of this wire can then be trimmed if the loop is to be placed into an arrangement, or left longer if it is to be taped to a posy or bouquet.

3 The loop with tail is made in a similar manner, but leaving the end of the ribbon as a tail before looping the ribbon and wiring.

choose to use this method, there are several ways to implement it. Firstly, you can stick your paste onto the cake directly, either with a little water, gum arabic glue or royal icing. Be very careful to cut your wires when arranging, so that they only go into the paste and avoid the cake surface – under no circumstances push wires directly into the cake. Secondly, so that the display can be more easily removed, you can make a plaque of sugarpaste, pastillage or flower (gum) paste which can then be stuck to the cake with royal icing. The flower paste or oasis is then attached to that. Or you can stick a tiny cakeboard to the top of your cake with just a few dots of royal icing so that it stays in position, and attach the paste or oasis to this.

With all these methods, the removal of the arrangement is the same. Take a thin palette knife and gently slide it under the board, plaque or paste. The arrangement should come away easily; carefully slide it to the edge of the cake and lift it away. Have ready a larger cakeboard or container with a little royal icing, and reposition on this.

4 Ribbon trails to finish posies and bouquets are simply composed of several lengths of ribbon, typically 30 to 45cm (12 to 18″). Group them together in the centre, and wind a long wire around the middle to hold them together and to double the number of tails. This is then wired in as the final piece of your posy or bouquet.

The final method of placing the flowers in position on the top of a cake is the use of a special 'posy pick'. This is a thin plastic container which is inserted into the cake itself and into which the flowers are placed. This prevents the wires coming into direct contact with the cake itself.

Should you decide to use this method, you must be very careful to ensure the pick is absolutely clean. I would certainly wash it in very hot water and then soak it in alcohol such as gin or vodka before inserting it into the cake. When the flowers are removed, you have to decide what to do if you wish to keep the cake. If you remove the pick, a mould may grow in the hole and the cake will be spoiled. Since you have inserted a sterile pick into a sterile medium, it might be just as well to leave the pick in place until the cake is finally cut.

This book shows flowers displayed only on the surfaces of cakes, and I personally find that I do not need picks at all.

A posy will most probably be displayed lying down, as it could only be properly viewed from above if presented in a vase. If you do plan to show your posy flat, find a small piece of foam and cover it with some co-ordinating material. This will protect the bottom flowers from breakage and give a pleasant base to your arrangement.

Remember, whatever method of presentation you decide on, ensure that you explain it fully to any recipient of the cake so that they can treat it appropriately.

PROPS AND CONTAINERS

You can get many ideas for containers and vases in which to arrange your projects just browsing around florist's shops and stores. Moulds can also be used to make little containers of your own, using pastillage, flower (gum) paste or mexican paste. A popular mould found in cake decorating supply shops is the bell mould, which come in a variety of sizes, and many shapes of little fluted tart tins which can also make useful moulds. You can easily cut out various shapes of plaques from paste, which are convenient for attaching directly to cakes or onto a cakeboard. There are many tiny cakeboards available nowadays that lend themselves to all sorts of shapes of arrangement. Available in the traditional silver, gold and red, possible shapes include round, square, oval and heart, available in 10 to 15cm (4 to 6″) sizes.

For competition work, gifts or special arrangements, there are several ideas you can employ for props and containers. For table decorations, I particularly like using octagonal mirrors with bevelled edges, which are quite unusual for display. I have also put sugar flowers into some little baskets that I found in a floristry supply shop. These particular items have given a great deal of pleasure, I have found, and are ideal little presents to keep in china cabinets or on little shelves.

A picture frame is another idea I particularly like, as it is fully enclosed and so protects the flowers, and is an ideal way to present your flowers as a gift. If you hide a silicon bag in the arrangement, the flowers should keep in a container indefinitely.

It should be borne in mind that sugar flowers are much heavier than fresh flowers or even silk flowers, so any container used must be stable enough to take the weight of the flowers without overbalancing. Some manufacturers make specially designed containers and stands particularly for cake decoration, using materials such as glass and perspex (plexiglass) so that the container does not detract from the flowers; these are also quite safe to place on your cake.

There are many artificial ornaments that can be used to enhance your floral arrangements. Stems of pearls can look very attractive, for instance, when wired in with a bouquet. Ribbon loops and small artificial fans or bunches of sparkly stamens can all be incorporated to good effect. Your use of these is entirely dependent on your own taste but my advice is to use them selectively and in limited quantities, as to overdo them will diminish the effect of the main attraction, namely the flowers you have made and arranged.

Above: A range of props and containers.

Round Arrangements

The round arrangement is a uniform dome-shape, with the items radiating from a centre point. Begin by placing background materials, i.e. leaves, horizontally into the paste then position the central flower upright. By doing this, you will establish the shape and height of your arrangement. Keep within the perimeters of this and work in rows of decreasing length, alternating the colours, up to the centre flower. Add final filler flowers and ribbon loops only after you are satisfied with the positioning of your main flowers, and be sure that the colour is well dispersed throughout the arrangement.

Victorian Posy

These posies make wonderful gifts. A Victorian posy in co-ordinating colours could be presented alongside a wedding cake to decorate the table. Here, perhaps, two would look good. Smaller Victorian posies look pleasing just placed onto a cake.

My Victorian posy is made up of burgundy rose buds, pine cones, cream-coloured spray carnations, filler flowers and ribbon loops, using a pale green rose leaf as a backing to the colours. I wanted to make this posy have a true Victorian feel, so I chose burgundy-coloured rose buds as the main colour. I was showing my sister some pine cones I'd made for my Christmas projects and it was she who suggested I use these for the Victorian posy as the Victorians used to like dried fragrant flowers and foliage around their homes. The pine cones certainly work well with the colour scheme and are quite distinctive. It is possible to use flowers mixed 'freestyle' into this shape, but this would then be a loose posy rather than a Victorian posy.

REQUIREMENTS

20cm (8″) posy frill.

27 pale green rose leaves, using leaf or moss liquid colour for the paste and dusted with green petal dust, on 30 gauge wire.

16 burgundy rose buds with green calyx on 24 gauge wire.

18 cream spray carnations on 26 gauge wire – these can be coloured with a tiny touch of brown cream or ivory paste.

19 filler blossoms. For these white blossoms I used small red sparkle stamens and white paste on 28 gauge wire.

13 brown-coloured sugarpaste pine cones on 24 gauge wire.

several cream 1.5mm ribbon loops on 30 gauge wire.

1 cream ribbon trail, using 4 assorted lengths of 1.5mm ribbon, on 30 gauge wire (see page 15).

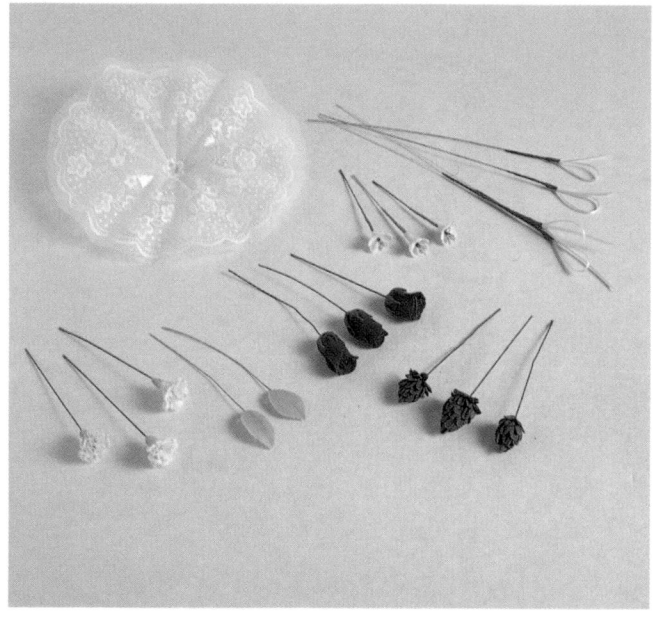

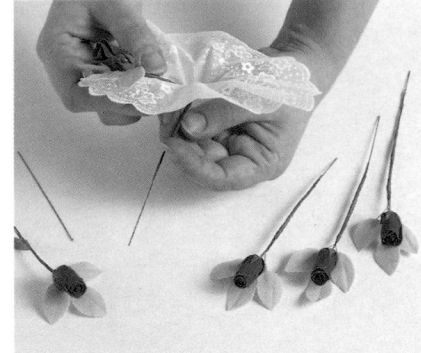

1 Take the posy frill and cut off the excess net around the edges to give an attractive finish. Cut four little nicks in the hole in the centre of the frill, to allow the hole to expand when being fitted to the posy: it is difficult to assess how thick your wires will be, and once the posy has been taped together, this allows for some adjustment in the base of the frill when it is fitted.

2 Take 3 rose leaves and tape them together, with the centre leaf slightly higher than the other two, which should be on the same level. Tape on a rose bud, slightly below the centre leaf. Tape on more 26 gauge wire if necessary, to give a stem of around 18 to 20 cm (7 to 8″) in length. Repeat to make 9 sprays.

Thread your stem through the posy frill, positioning the top leaf so that it overlaps the frill by 5mm to 1cm (¼ to ½″). Bend the wire underneath the frill at the exact point where it meets the netting. Remove the wire from the frill and reserve for later. Repeat the procedure to bend all 9 sprays.

3 Take a rose bud and 3 carnations and tape them together, with the carnations on the same level but all lower than the rose bud. In between each carnation, on the same level, tape a filler blossom, 3 in all.

Slightly lower, tape a row of 6 pine cones. Beneath each pine cone, tape a carnation, and then in between each carnation, place a rose bud.

4 Now take your 9 leaf and bud sprays, 1 or 2 at a time, and using the bend already made, tape these around your stem. There will be quite a gap, but once you have the sprays placed and taped in a circle around your centrepiece, you will begin to see how the dome-shaped arrangement is formed. No flower should be sticking out in any one row further than the one below it or to the side of it, and each row should be slightly lower than the last, and slightly further out.

5 Beneath each carnation and above one of the outside rose buds, tape a row of pine cones, 6 in all. In between this row of pine cones, at the same level, work in a row of 6 filler blossoms. Finally, position a row of alternate carnations and blossoms.

When looking at the posy from the side, it should be domed in shape. It should have uniform rows going around, and the rows from top to bottom should fall into a regular pattern.

6 Thread in the wired ribbon loops to fill the gaps. They should not be in great evidence: they are simply the garnish to complete the arrangement and as such should be used only at the end to finish off. When added carefully, ribbons can enhance your work and create a beautiful effect.

Wire on your ribbon trail, remembering that wherever this is positioned will be the bottom of the arrangement, as the posy is presented with the ribbons hanging down.

7 Fit the posy frill on the back of the arrangement. You may be surprised to see that it is hardly in evidence, but this is the correct use of the frill in a Victorian posy. It is used only as a backing so that when you look through the arrangement, the posy frill will fill in any gaps.

Tape the back of the stem with white stem wrap and then carefully cover with ribbon in a complementary colour. Bend the wire if you need to for your own presentation.

To finish off, attach a ribbon bow at the top of the stem behind the arrangement. Using the principle described, you can make larger or smaller posies, and of course any variations of colours and flowers you like.

Two-Tier Golden Wedding Cake I

This two-tier petal-shaped cake uses 2 separate shapes of arrangement. For the top I have used a round arrangement, which I felt was appropriate for this project, although another good shape to use would be a crescent, which would leave you a space to pipe on names or greetings. The matching asymmetrical arrangements on the sides are given on **page 53**.

I have made this particular design on many occasions and have found it to be very popular and versatile. The first time I made it, for a twenty-first birthday celebration, I used pink flowers. On other occasions, I was asked to adapt it for a Silver Wedding anniversary, and then for a two-tier wedding cake. By just changing the colour of the flowers, you can use this design for other celebrations.

REQUIREMENTS

7.5 cm (3″) cakeboard.

25g (1oz) lump of rolled fondant (sugarpaste).

6 leaf and moss green coloured rose leaves, dusted with leaf green, on 30 gauge wire.

12 sprays of 3 medium plunger blossoms with bud stamen, on 26 gauge wire.

13 cream- or lemon-coloured rose buds with leaf green calyx, on 24 gauge wire.

12 white blossoms with fine yellow stamens, on 26 gauge wire.

10 sprays of 3 blue-coloured forget-me-nots on 26 gauge wire.

Several white pulled blossoms on 26 gauge wire.

Several pale lemon or cream 1.5mm ribbon loops on 26 gauge wire.

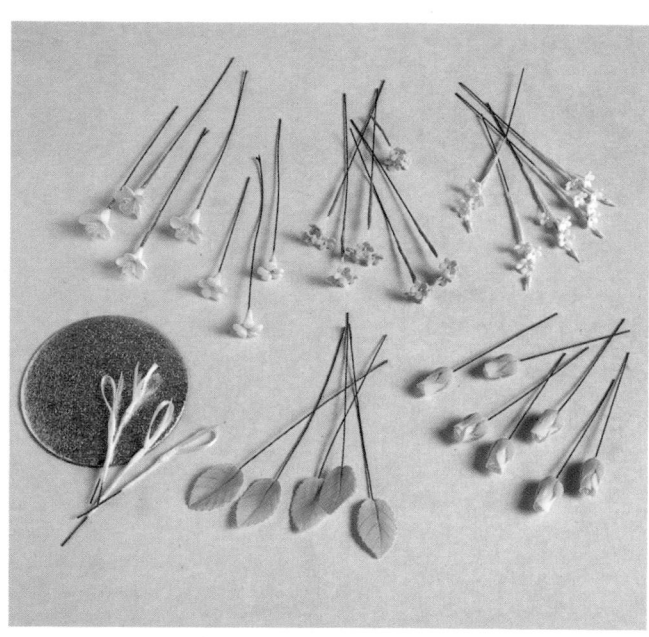

1 Position the cakeboard onto the cake, securing with royal icing: a round arrangement looks better in the centre. Press on a ball of worked rolled fondant (sugarpaste), which will form the oasis for the flowers.

I use the petal shape of the cake to give me my guideline for positioning the 6 leaves. Trimming wires as necessary, place 1 leaf in line with the centre of each petal. Over each leaf, position a spray of plunger blossoms.

2 In between each leaf, place the remaining plunger blossom sprays. Next, position 6 of the rose buds, 1 over each leaf and blossom spray. Set 1 rose bud upright in the centre of the whole arrangement. This will set the height of your arrangement.

3 Taking the height of the top rose and the circular edge you have made as your perimeters, arrange all the other flowers to form a dome shape.

In between the first 6 rose buds, place 6 of the white blossoms with yellow stamens over the blossoms. Above each of these, place another rose bud. In between and slightly above these rose buds, position another yellow-stamen blossom.

4 Use the forget-me-nots in an evenly spaced ring of 6 bunches around the base of the arrangement, and bring the colour up into the top of the arrangement by placing the final 4 bunches around the central rose bud.

5 Finally, fill in with the remaining filler flowers and ribbon loops.

The illustrated cake is a 20cm (8″) petal tier on top of a 30cm (12″) petal cake, placed on a thin 30cm (12″) gold cakeboard. The cake is covered in white rolled fondant (sugarpaste) and decorated with white garrett double frills (ruffles), with embroidery piping above. A shell trail has been piped around the base of the cakes. For details of how to make the asymmetrical side arrangements, see page 53.

Crescent Arrangements

The crescent shape is made up of a curved shape, equal on both sides. The colour should always be dispersed throughout the crescent and one way of doing this is to graduate the size of flowers used towards the centre. Always start with the outline of leaves and use the shapes thus created as your guidelines.

Generally, the crescent is not a good shape to use if you need some height, but it is ideal for cake decorating, particularly if your cake needs to be transported, since high arrangements can be difficult to accommodate in a box. Of course, a complete arrangement in the crescent shape lends itself to almost any cake shape and for almost any occasion. It would be delightful on the tiers of a wedding cake or simply on the top tier. It also leaves you plenty of space on your cake for greetings and candles.

Christening Cake

When I lived in Texas, my lady doctor took a great interest in my hobby. We became very friendly and when she had her little girl, I made a Christening cake for her, similar to this one. She was so delighted with it that I thought I would repeat it here. I've dedicated it to my niece who was born while we were out in California and unable to take part in her Christening.

This use of the crescent shape is particularly elegant for a Christening cake, using the sugarpaste crib as a centrepiece. For a different occasion, you could of course carry the flowers all the way round and leave out the crib. I think you could also get away with this design for a boy's cake, using pale blue and white flowers or perhaps just soft greens. If you do not want to make a whole cake for a Christening party but feel you would like to offer something special, this arrangement would look adorable worked onto an oval cake board, and just given as a gift to the parents.

REQUIREMENTS

12 rose leaves, coloured with a touch of leaf green, on 30 gauge wire.

16 white sprays of 3 medium plunger blossoms with white bud stamen, on 26 gauge wire.

10 white apple blossoms, dusted with plain or lustre pink petal dust, on 26 gauge wire.

8 ivory-coloured miniature orchids on 26 gauge wire.

Several pale pink 1.5mm ribbon loops on 26 gauge wire.

10 ivory-coloured rose buds with leaf green calyx on 24 gauge wire.

7.5cm (3") cakeboard.

25g (1oz) lump of flower (gum) paste.

Sugarpaste baby in crib.

Several white gypsophila stamens, taped in 4s on 26 gauge wire.

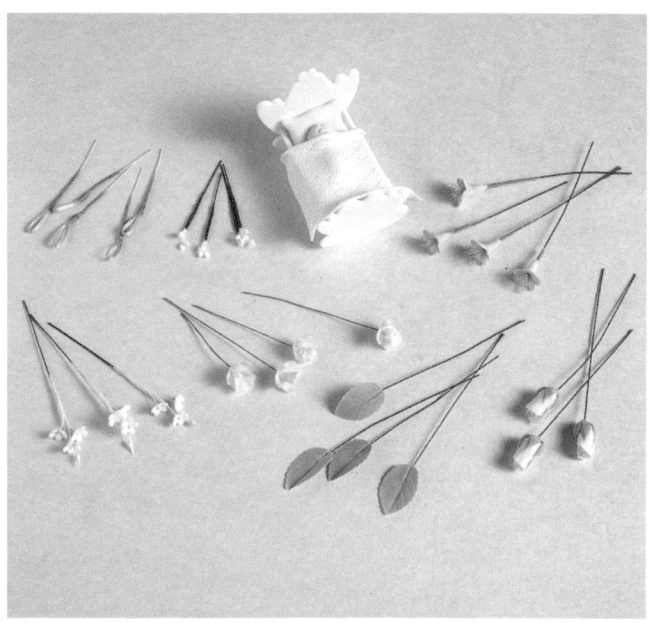

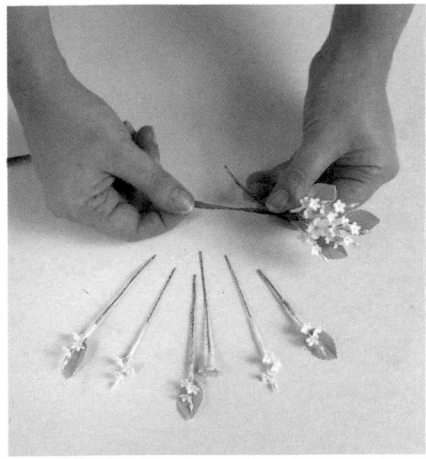

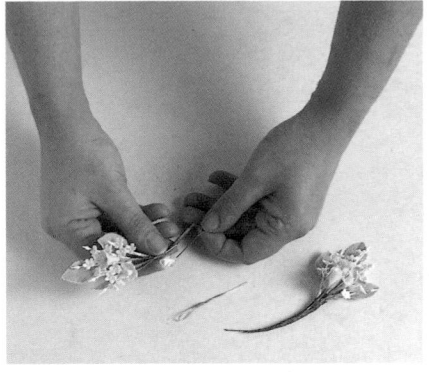

1 Tape a leaf and blossom spray together, and repeat to make 3 double sprays. Tape so that one is flanked on both sides by the other 2, and position a blossom spray in the gap between each. Tape an apple blossom on top of the stems in the centre, leaving the leaf and blossoms showing.

2 Attach a miniature orchid to the *right* of the spray, with a ribbon loop tucked in behind. Coming down into the centre of the spray, tape on a rose bud and a pale pink ribbon loop. Curve the spray slightly, away from the orchid in direction, and set to one side.

Repeat the above, in exactly the same way, but position the miniature orchid to the *left* of the spray and curve it the opposite direction.

3 Place the miniature cakeboard onto the cake, securing with a few drops of royal icing. Work about 40–50g (1½–2oz) of flower (gum) paste until it is soft. Flatten and shape and fix to the board with a little water.

Place the crib in the centre, adding enough paste or royal icing to the underside so that it stays put when all is dry. There should be some paste showing under the crib on either side, into which the flowers will be arranged.

4 Take the 2 sprays and position them into the paste either side of the crib. As this is an even-sided arrangement, remember that what you do to one side should also be repeated on the other. The sprays should both be curving inwards, following the curve of your cake, and the ends should be an equal distance from the crib.

5 Tape all the remaining plunger blossom sprays onto individual leaves. Continue to create your shape by positioning the leaf-and-blossom sprays, smoothly following the curve of the arrangement. Place 2 leaves at the base at the back on each side, and 1 at the front. (The arrangement has its wider curve at the back, so more leaves are needed there.)

6 Position 4 rose buds on each side, offset from each other in a zigzag pattern. In between these, and in a similar pattern, position the remaining 4 apple blossoms on each side. This disperses the colour throughout the arrangement.

7 Now fill in with 4 miniature orchids on each side. Use the pale pink ribbon loops to separate the ivory colour where flowers of the same colour are next to each other, and to highlight and fill in spaces.

Finally, by adding the wired gypsophila stamens, a feathery feminine look is added to the arrangement. Insert these with the aid of surgical hemostats or tweezers.

Illustrated is a 25cm (10″) round cake on a 32.5cm (13″) cakeboard. It is covered in pale pink rolled fondant (sugarpaste) and decorated with pale pink garrett scalloped frills (ruffles) and white piped lace. The outside of the board is embossed, and a white snail trail is piped, interspersed with pink dots, around the base of the cake. A length of 1.5mm pink ribbon and piped pink lettering completes the effect.

33

Semi-Crescent Arrangements

The semi-crescent is a reversed comma-shaped arrangement with the bulk of its flowers towards the top, trailing off into an elongated tail. I feel that a heart-shaped cake lends itself particularly well to this arrangement, although rounds, ovals and in fact any curved cake will accommodate the design just as beautifully.

Though the semi-crescent is similar in structure to the crescent shape, one curved side is kept shorter than the other during construction. This gives a mass of flowers near the top that tails down the longest curved point. You can make your tail go to the left or to the right, but the shape you create should resemble a comma.

If wiring the crescent shape rather than making an arrangement directly on a cake, you will find that less flowers are needed.

Valentine Cake

On February 14, 271 AD, the emperor Claudius put to death a young priest called Valentine for defying an edict that forbade weddings. Legend has it that the emperor thought that single men made better soldiers, and Valentine had been carrying out weddings in secret. The martyred Saint Valentine has lived on in romantic hearts through the centuries that followed. The Victorians developed the custom of sending love notes to their sweethearts on February 14 every year, and the tradition of Valentine's Day evolved.

For this special Valentine cake, I chose the semi-crescent shaped arrangement. Using the semi-crescent in this way requires many more flowers than a wired corsage would, but the latter would look just as pleasing placed on a cake. If you are pressed for time, you could wire the arrangement, but if, like myself, you like to see lots of detail and if you are making the cake for someone special, I think it is worth the extra effort to make this semi-crescent display. This colour scheme would also be ideal for a ruby wedding celebration cake.

REQUIREMENTS

16 sprays of 3 medium plunger blossoms with green stamens and 1 bud stamen, taped on 26 gauge wire.

16 pale leaf green-coloured rose leaves on 30 gauge wire.

2 rose centres, coloured and wired as above.

13–14 white filler flowers with red sparkle stamens, on 26 gauge wire.

12–15 1.5mm red ribbon loops on 26 gauge wire.

12–13 opening rose buds, coloured and wired as above.

50g (2oz) lump of flower (gum) paste or sugarpaste.

5 red-coloured full red roses, with leaf green-coloured calyx, on 24 gauge wire.

Several gypsophila, made from 4 stamens, taped together at varying heights.

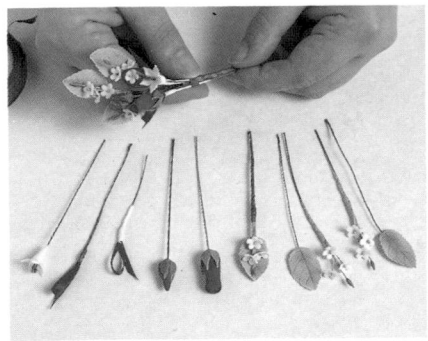

1 First, tape each blossom spray to a rose leaf ready to assemble in the arrangements. Then, tape 1 rose centre to a leaf-and-blossom spray. Add a leaf-and-blossom either side.

To the right, add a filler flower and a ribbon loop. In the centre, tape an opening rose bud, then add another ribbon loop to the left. Curve this spray towards the right, set to one side and proceed to the second spray arrangement.

2 Take a rose centre and tape it to a leaf-and-blossom spray. Add 2 more leaf-and-blossoms either side.

Tape a ribbon loop and a filler flower to the centre. Position an opening rose bud to the right, then add another opening rose bud in the centre. Continue with a leaf-and-blossom on either side, then add a ribbon loop and a filler flower to the right. Curve this spray towards the left and set aside.

3 Place the flower (gum) or sugarpaste onto the cake where you will assemble your arrangement. You can either fix the paste directly to the cake with a little water, egg white or gum arabic glue, or you can make a plaque from pastillage, flower (gum) paste or sugarpaste, fix this to the cake with a few drops of royal icing and fix the lump of paste to this. If you are copying this arrangement, and wish to place it on a miniature cakeboard, be aware that I have found the smallest cakeboard available to be a little too big for this project, so it may show a little.

Take the smaller of the 2 sprays that you have made and position it at the top in the 12 o'clock position. Place the larger spray opposite, at the 6 o'clock position. Both sprays should curve inwards, into the arrangement.

4 On the inside (right), position 3 leaf-and-blossom sprays, remembering to cut off excess wire. They need to be kept in line with the arrangement as always.

Similarly, place 5 leaf-and-blossom sprays to create a wide outside curve, falling in line with the top and bottom sprays.

5 Take the full roses and place them into the paste in a curving line following the outside leaves: this should require 4. Place the fifth and final rose offset to the side between the 2 centre roses. Prop up the roses with added bits of paste if necessary to achieve the desired position.

6 Now that the main flowers have been placed and your shape created, go around the outside and position the remaining opening rose buds to outline the arrangement with colour.

7 Carefully fill in with the remaining filler flowers, ribbon loops and gypsophila.

The arrangement is displayed on a 20cm (8″) heart-shaped cake, placed on a 25cm (10″) heart-shaped cakeboard. Both are covered in white rolled fondant (sugarpaste), and the edge of the board is embossed with hearts. A shell border is piped around the base of the cake, and a name piped on top. 23mm (1″) red ribbon encircles the cake and 9mm (³⁄₈″) ribbon encircles the board.

Jade Corsage

Any shade of blue is rather difficult to use in any great amount when decorating food. There is nothing edible that I can think of which comes in blue, so using this colour in excess would probably put off many people from eating the item you are trying to decorate! However, when doing wedding work, you may be asked to include blue in your decoration. I suggest that you use it sparingly, just as a highlight rather than a main colour.

Here I have used jade, really as a little fantasy, in a semi-crescent corsage. You will of course be able to make up this design with any colour flowers you wish.

REQUIREMENTS

17 leaves, coloured with blue and green petal dust (mixed with a little white vegetable fat), and dusted when dry with jade petal dust. On 30 gauge wire.

9 sprays of 3 white medium plunger blossoms with 1 bud stamen, taped on 26 gauge wire.

5 carnations, coloured as for the leaves, on 26 gauge wire.

8 or 9 1.5mm jade-coloured ribbon loops on 28 gauge wire.

6 or 7 white pulled blossoms, the centres dusted with yellow petal dust, on 28 gauge wire.

2 white cattleya orchids, dusted with yellow; on 30 gauge wire for the petals, 26 gauge wire for the throat.

9mm jade-coloured ribbon bow.

1 Take a leaf and tape onto it a stem of blossoms. Repeat to make a total of 9. Take 1 leaf-and-blossom spray and tape a leaf either side of its stem. Add a white pulled blossom over each leaf, and a carnation in the centre.

A little further down the stem, on either side, tape 1 of the prepared leaf-and-blossoms. Over each of those, tape a ribbon loop. Set this starter spray aside and make another in exactly the same way.

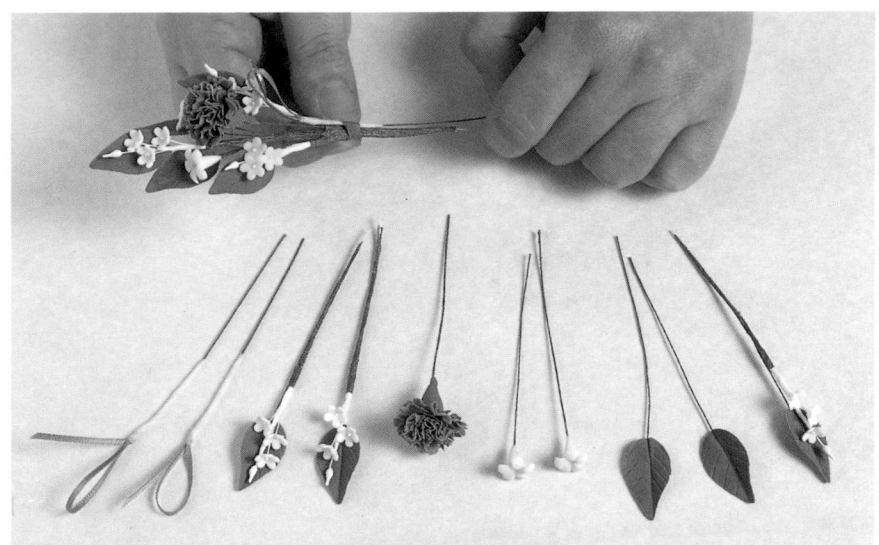

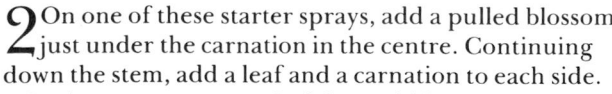

2 On one of these starter sprays, add a pulled blossom just under the carnation in the centre. Continuing down the stem, add a leaf and a carnation to each side.

In the centre, tape on 1 of the orchids. You can add a little extra wire at this stage to make the corsage easier to handle, if you need to.

3 Bend the wire of the spray back, at right angles. Now take the second starter spray (the other half of the corsage), bend back its wire at right angles and tape it to the first section.

41

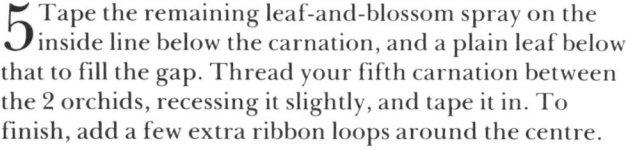

4 Position your second orchid opposite your first orchid, facing in the opposite direction. Carefully curve the top half of the arrangement to make a semi-crescent.

Following the outside line, tape in 2 leaf-and-blossom stems, plus 1 leaf and a pulled blossom in between these.

5 Tape the remaining leaf-and-blossom spray on the inside line below the carnation, and a plain leaf below that to fill the gap. Thread your fifth carnation between the 2 orchids, recessing it slightly, and tape it in. To finish, add a few extra ribbon loops around the centre.

6 Bend the wire stem forward and down so that the corsage can lie flat. Then, if you wish, add a bow to the top of the stem to finish off.

The corsage is presented on a 20cm (8″) hexagonal cakeboard, covered in white rolled fondant (sugarpaste) and with an edge embossed. 9mm (⅜″) jade ribbon surrounds the board. Alternatively, the corsage can be laid directly onto a cake.

Symmetrical Arrangements

Arranging flowers in a symmetrical shape is very traditional. It is mainly front-facing, meaning that all flowers and leaves are presented facing forward, since the arrangement will have a backing of some sort. (In floristry, this is usually a wall.) Here, I have used both a cake to back the arrangement and a greetings card made of pastillage. Anything will be fine as long as it hides the mechanics of the arrangement at the back.

The shape is achieved by placing foliage around the back, shaping it to a point at the top and following down the sides to form a triangular shape. The two sloping sides should be equal in length at this stage and identical to each other. Remember to position foliage horizontally at the front, and position your main flowers to give main height and so that they are dispersed evenly throughout the arrangement. Remember these need to be relatively symmetrical, too. When finishing off with filler flowers, recess them to give added depth to your work.

The floral arrangements are shown on a 30cm (12″) square cake, placed on a 35cm (14″) and then a 45cm (18″) cakeboard for added protection. These are covered with white rolled fondant (sugarpaste) and are decorated with embossed edges and a large piped snail trail border around the base of the cake. Pearl and lace ribbons encircle the cake, and the boards are edged with 9mm (⅜″) bright pink ribbon. Details on how to make the bridal bouquet are given on page 58.

Greetings Card

This small greetings card arrangement is eminently suitable for the top of any celebration cake, or would be charming used as an alternative to a regular birthday, anniversary, Christmas or special occasion card of any kind. The flowers are arranged in a symmetrical shape, but you could also use an asymmetrical arrangement.

The greetings card is made with tight rosebuds and tiny spray carnations. It is placed on an oval 10cm (4″) board for presentation, but it could also be placed under a glass dome if you can find one large enough.

To make the basic greetings card, first cut out two oblongs (using a card template or cutter) from petal paste or pastillage. In one, cut out an oval hole, slightly lower than the centre to allow the arrangement to fall through. When dry, glue together at an angle with royal icing, and pipe pink embroidery around the hole and any message inside. Secure to a 10cm (4″) cakeboard with royal icing.

REQUIREMENTS

1 white petal paste or pastillage greetings card, 9cm (3½″) oblong.

25–40g (1–1½oz) lump of flower (gum) paste.

11 small pale green-coloured leaves on 30 gauge wire.

11 small sprays of 3 brown and pink-coloured plunger blossoms with 1 bud stamen, on 26 gauge wire.

7 cream-coloured rose buds, with pale green calyx, dusted with a mixture of pink petal dust and cornflour to give a peachy look. On 24 gauge wire.

7 small brown and pink-coloured spray carnations, on 26 gauge wire.

Several pulled white filler flowers on 26 gauge wire.

Dark orange-coloured 1.5mm ribbon loops on 26 gauge wire.

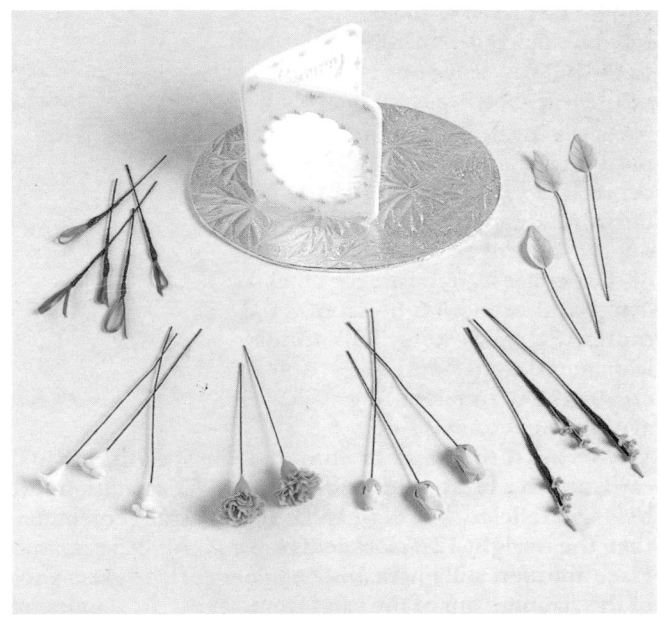

Bridal Bouquet of Cattleya Orchids

This wired arrangement could be described as pea~~r~~ or teardrop in shape – it is a traditional brida~~l~~ bouquet shape. It would lie well on the top of a cak~~e~~ as long as the wires are cut down or bent flat. T~~o~~ arrange directly onto the top tier of a wedding cake put an oasis of flower (gum) paste on top of the cake and arrange flowers directly into this. (Thi~~s~~ way, there would be no insertion of wires into the cake itself.)

Alternatively, one could reproduce a bride's fres~~h~~ bouquet in a sugar arrangement as a memento o~~f~~ the occasion. This particular shape can be scale~~d~~

Handwritten note (overlay):

Blue Flowers (made)
5 large.
4 smaller.
8 white pulled flowers.
White plunger sprays – 6
9 violets
10 plunger sprays – red.
+ 12
Carnations large 7
11 smaller 14

REQUIREMENTS

Ivy leaves: all are made in cream on 30 gauge wire and painted in varying shades of moss green to give a variegated effect. You will need:
5 very small ivy leaves.
17 medium ivy leaves.
14 large ivy leaves.
9 sprays of fuchsia-coloured plunger blossoms, wired together in groups of 1 bud and 3 flowers, on 26 gauge wire.
1 stephanotis bud on 26 gauge wire.

3 or more stephanotis flowers on 26 gauge wire.
7 apple blossoms, 5 with buds. These were made in white and dusted with a mixture of pink petal dust and cornflour to lighten it a little. Use brown tape on 26 gauge wire.
5 white carnations on 26 gauge wire.
Several shocking pink 3mm ribbon loops on 28 gauge wire.
4 pulled filler flowers on 26

gau~~ge~~ wire, d~~usted~~
pin~~k~~ with bright pink
peta~~l~~ dust in the petals.
3 or mo~~re~~ white freesias on
26 ga~~uge~~ wires.
5 fuchsia-coloured cattleya orchids; the petals on 30 gauge wire, the throat on 26 gauge wire.
7 sprays of lily of the valley on 26 gauge wire.
5 stems of pearls.
1 bright pink ribbon trail on 30 gauge wire (page 15).
1cm (½″) white florists' or satin ribbon.

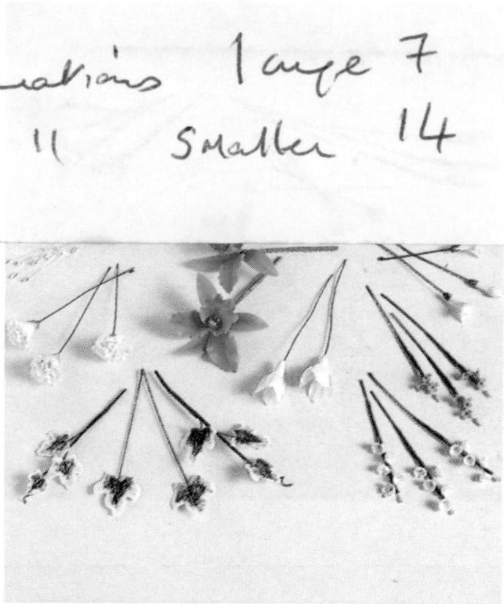

1 First make 5 small ivy sprays: take a piece of dark green 30 gauge further down, tape a medium-sized ivy leaf. Finally, on the opposite side, tape another the tip of the se of the last ivy approximately u spread them u will not be around the

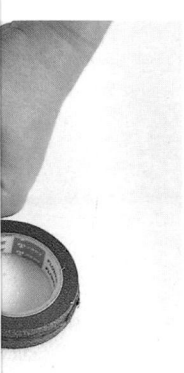

2 Make 7 medium ivy sprays by repeating all of the above steps, but using a medium ivy leaf in place of the small one at the top and 2 large leaves in place of the medium ones on the sides.

To 5 of these ivy sprays, tape a small blossom spray and to this add extra lengths of 24 gauge wire – half a complete wire length will be about right.

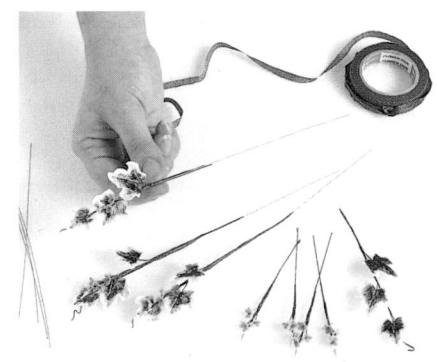

N.B. You may need to tape extra wire to some flowers to make them easier to insert into your work. The lily of the valley particularly will need extra lengths, as will the final orchids and the filler flowers.

3 Start wiring up the bridal bouquet. Take one of the small ivy sprays and tape onto it one of the small blossom sprays. About 2cm (1″) further up to the right, tape a stephanotis bud. Slightly higher and to the left, tape a stephanotis flower. Then, to the right and still higher, tape an apple blossom.

To the left and quite further back along the wire, tape the second spray of small ivy leaves. This second spray of ivy should be situated so that it starts to widen the arrangement slightly. (You are trying to start a line that gradually widens out as you work your way up the bouquet arrangement. The first point will be your first ivy leaf spray and the second and subsequent points will be the tips of the other ivy sprays. It is the correct position of these sprays that will create the shape of your overall arrangement.)

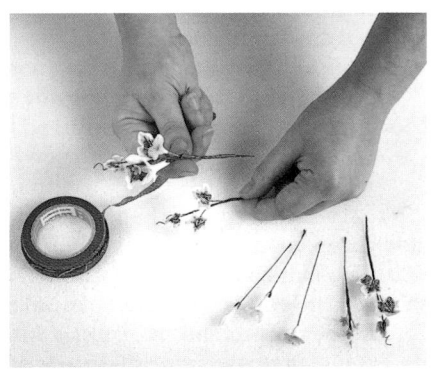

10 Now fill in with your remaining flowers, the stephanotis, freesias, carnations, apple blossoms and pulled fillers. These should be tucked underneath the main flowers to give the arrangement depth and texture. Do not overfill the gaps. The approach is, in modern floristry, that you need to leave room for the butterflies to fly through. Rather a charming thought!

Only now do you go back and thread in simple ribbon loops. You do not need to overdo this – just add a few to highlight your arrangement. Ribbon is a wonderful accessory but should not overshadow the charm of the flowers you have made.

Should you wish to add a little touch of 'something else', now is the time to do it. Here, I have inserted about 5 stems of pearls. Again, don't overdo it – it is the sugar flowers that are the attraction.

11 Now take your ribbon trail, made from 4 lengths of ribbon which you have folded in half and wired together to give a tassle of 8 ribbon strands. Tape it on so that the ribbon falls beneath the arrangement. To enhance the effect, you can cut the ribbon to different lengths.

To finish off, cut your stem to the required length, overtaping it neatly with white floral tape, and then, should you wish, with wider white satin ribbon. A bow may be placed at the top of the stem if desired – this of course is only necessary if there is a chance of the back of the bouquet being exposed. It would not apply if you intend to place the arrangement directly onto a cake.

4 Fill in with bunches of the forget-me-nots, remembering to space them evenly so that you don't get flowers of the same colour next to each other.

Position the ribbon loops sparingly, but evenly, throughout the arrangement to highlight.

5 Turn the cake around and insert a couple of filler flowers, forget-me-nots and ribbon loops behind the first leaf at the top, so that the view from behind the arrangement is pleasant, and so that you don't see a lump of paste! Once the paste in which the arrangement has been made is set, and the cake is ready to cut, it should be a simple matter just to ease the whole arrangement from the corner and display it in a suitable container, if desired.

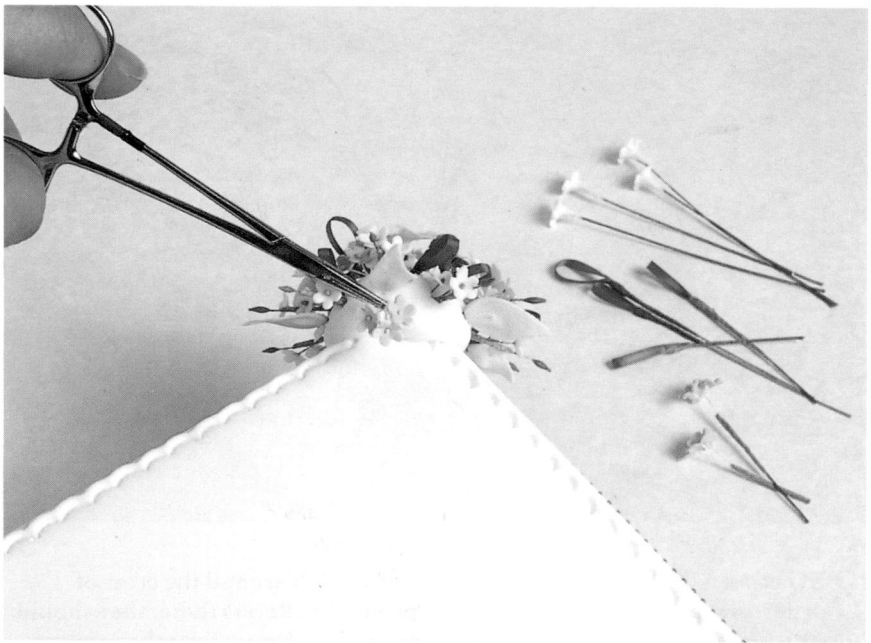

The bouquets are arranged in the corners of a 30cm (12″) square cake on a 37.5cm (15″) cakeboard. These are covered in white rolled fondant (sugarpaste) and are decorated with crimped edges and a closed double scallop shell border around the base of the cake. Purple 9mm (⅜″) crimped ribbon encircles the cake and board, and a name has been piped on.

4 Take the pine cones and position them evenly throughout the arrangement. Keep within your perimeters of height and shape, and do not group them closely together.

5 In the same way, take the holly berries and place these evenly throughout the arrangement. Carry the colour to all points and recess the berries beneath the level of the other foliage to give the arrangement depth. Fill in evenly with the variegated ivy leaves.

6 Finally, insert the remaining 10–12 single medium holly leaves and the golden ribbon loops.

The display is shown on a 20 × 25cm (8 × 10″) octagonal cake on a 30 × 35cm (12 × 14″) silver cakeboard. The cake is covered in white rolled fondant (sugarpaste), and the board is edged with 9mm (⅜″) forest green ribbon, piped above and below with a scalloped line. The side decoration (designed by Adrian Westrope) has a piped stem trail in Christmas green overlaid with an appliqué effect of piped spruce and paste pine cones, holly and ivy leaves.